George Cooper, Harrison Millard

Chaplet of Original Hymns and Songs

George Cooper, Harrison Millard

Chaplet of Original Hymns and Songs

ISBN/EAN: 9783337296728

Printed in Europe, USA, Canada, Australia, Japan

Cover: Foto ©Thomas Meinert / pixelio.de

More available books at **www.hansebooks.com**

"Suffer little Children to come unto me."

THE CHAPLET

— OF —

ORIGINAL HYMNS AND SONGS,

Christmas and Easter Carols,

CONCERT EXERCISES, &c.

FOR SUNDAY SCHOOLS,

AND SHORT OPENING PIECES AND CHANTS

FOR CHURCH CHOIRS.

Words by GEORGE COOPER.

MUSIC BY

Harrison Millard.

BOSTON:

G. D. RUSSELL & COMPANY.

N. B.—All the words in the "CHAPLET," excepting the Chants, are Original Copyright Matter. Parties desiring to use them on Sunday School programmes for Anniversaries, or on Christmas, must first obtain written permission from H. MILLARD, of New York, otherwise they will incur the penalty of the law.

Entered according to Act of Congress, A. D. 1873, by HARRISON MILLARD, in the Office of the Librarian of Congress at Washington.

GILES & GOULD, Music Printers, 69 Washington Street, Boston.

3. What shall we care for sorrows past—
   In that blest home where Angels dwell?
Rest never-ending crowns us at last,—
   In that blest home where Angels dwell!
There shall our feet be done with their roving,
   There shall our songs in rapture swell!
There shall we see our Saviour so loving,—
   In that blest home where Angels dwell!

Haste ye Nations to adore Him.

3. He is King of Kings forever!
   Sing His love, from shore to shore!
  Let your praises, like a river,
   Flow to Him forevermore!
  Haste, ye nations, to adore Him!
   Swell the everlasting song!
  All ye people bow before Him!
   Earth and sea His praise prolong!

Entered, according to Act of Congress, A. D. 1872, by H. MILLARD, in the Office of the Librarian of Congress at Washington.

The Gates Ajar.

Entered, according to Act of Congress, A. D. 1872, by H MILLARD, in the Office of the Librarian of Congress at Washington.

Raise the banner of the Cross.

1. Raise the ban-ner of the Cross, And set our an-thems ring-ing! March we on thro' pain and loss, All dan-gers we de-fy! Faith our ar-mor! still we're sing-ing, Un-to God our trib-ute bringing; On-ward ev-er! Fal-ter nev-er! Sol-diers! Raise the ban-ner of the Cross, we'll con-quer or die!

2.
All around us, see! the foe
  Is marshalled to assail us!
Sin shall fall at every blow,
  And darksome Error fly!
Jesus leads us! what can fail us?
Holy Angels proudly hail us!
  Onward ever! Falter never!
    Soldiers!
Raise the banner of the Cross, we'll conquer or die!

3.
We are battling for the Right,
  And Wrong shall ever fear us!
God will aid us with His might,
  And all our needs supply!
He will guide us, He will cheer us!
He will bless and linger near us!
  Onward ever! Falter never!
    Soldiers!
Raise the banner of the Cross, we'll conquer or **die!**

Entered according to Act of Congress, A. D. 1873, by H. MILLARD, in the Office of the Librarian of Congress, at Washington.

Be ye Joyful.

3. Be ye joyful for His goodness,—
For His earth so bright and fair!
Thank Him for our homes so happy,
And our dear ones nestled there!
Shout the story of His glory!—
God is reigning still on high!
Be ye joyful, little children!—
God the Father magnify!

Entered, according to Act of Congress, A.D. 1872, by H. MILLARD, in the Office of the Librarian of Congress at Washington.

3 Lest ye heed the Tempter's cry,
   Watch and pray!
Tho' your troubled hearts may sigh,
   Watch and pray!
Lo! the hour is close at hand,
We are near the Heavenly land:
Heed our loving Lord's command,
   Watch and pray!
   Watch and pray!

3 Take Him fondly unto your breast,—
   Let the Saviour in!
   He will give to the weary rest,—
   Let the Saviour in!
   Shall His summons be heard in vain?
   Shall we turn Him away again?—
   Ye who linger in doubt and pain,—
   Let the Saviour in!

Fight the Good Fight.

2 Fight the good fight nobly,
   Heed the Tempter not!
   In the march to Vict'ry
   Be our toils forgot!
   Onward still, and upward!
   Fear not slight nor frown!
   Soon, in joy and triumph,
   Ye shall wear the crown!
Cho.—Fight the good fight, &c.

Beyond the River.

Sweet Thoughts of Heaven.

As our Day.

Give!

He Leads us On.

A little Child shall Lead.

Semplice.

1. How sweet, how dear the hal-lowed spell That lin-gers round the words that fell, In gen-tle tones, from lips Di-vine! For-ev-er in our hearts they shine! O, not the great and not the wise Shall be the first, be-yond the skies! But in its good-ness, mild and fair, A lit-tle child shall lead us there! But in its goodness, mild and fair, A lit-tle child shall lead us there!

2. Our Sav-iour loved the chil-dren dear, He blessed them ev-er-more while here; He spoke to them in ac-cents mild, And lik-en'd Heav'n un-to a child! O, love the lit-tle ones we meet, And guide to Heav'n their gen-tle feet! For in its good-ness, mild and fair, A lit-tle child shall lead us there! For in its goodness, mild and fair, A lit-tle child shall lead us there!

Entered, according to Act of Congress, A.D. 1872, by H. MILLARD, in the Office of the Librarian of Congress at Washington.

Scatter Seed.

3.
Tho' thy toil should seem to fail,
  Scatter seed! Scatter seed!
Some may fall on stony ground,
Flower and blade are often found
In the clefts we little heed!
  Scatter seed! Scatter seed!

4.
Seed-time always dawns for thee,
  Scatter seed! Scatter seed!
Ope thy spirit's golden store,
Stretch thy furrows more and more;
God will give to thee thy meed!
  Scatter seed! Scatter seed!

Father, Take our Hands.

Sabbath Bells!

We'll soon be Home.

3 Wait but a little while,—
We'll soon be Home!
Jesus will on us smile,—
We'll soon be Home!
He will His comfort send,
He is our only Friend;
Trust Him unto the end,—
We'll soon be Home!

Little Pilgrims.

Moderato.

1. Lit-tle pilgrims, on our jour-ney, We are wand-'ring, day by day! All a-round us are temp-ta-tions, May we choose the bless-ed way! Gen-tle Sav-iour, kind-ly lead us, Suf-fer us to come to Thee! We are pil-grims, on our jour-ney, Trav'ling to E-ter-ni-ty!

2. Lit-tle pilgrims, proudly sing-ing, While we lin-ger here be-low; May our prais-es, ev-er ring-ing, Up to Heav'n in rap-ture flow! Should we fal-ter, be Thou near us, Lead us from the path of Wrong! Come and join us, wea-ry stran-ger, Come and join our pil-grim song!

CHORUS.

Lit-tle pilgrims! lit-tle pilgrims! Wand'rers in a des-ert land! Gen-tle Sav-iour, lov-ing Sav-iour, Homeward lead our pil-grim band!

Entered, according to Act of Congress, A.D. 1872, by H. MILLARD, in the Office of the Librarian of Congress at Washington.

The Sparrow's Fall.

Let us fold our Hands.

31

2. Saviour watching from the skies,
   Let Thy blessing on us fall!
   Through the gloom that round us lies,
   Father, keep and shelter all!
   Kindly take a little child
   In Thy sweet and holy care—
   Gentle Saviour, meek and mild,
   Let us fold our hands in prayer,—
   Fold our little hands in prayer!
   Let us fold our hands in prayer!

Entered, according to Act of Congress, A.D. 1872, by H MILLARD, in the Office of the Librarian of Congress at Washington.

Pray without Ceasing.

2 Pray for His guidance
  When doubts shall arise;
Never unheeded
  Your pitiful cries!
Strength to your bosom
  His mercy shall send;
Let our petitions
  In harmony blend!
Cho.—Pray to our Father, &c.

3 Pray, for the darkness
  Of night cometh on!
Pray till your labor
  Is over and done!
Pray till the warfare
  Of sin shall be o'er;
Pray to the Father
  Of all, evermore!
Cho.—Pray to our Father, &c.

2 When weary, we come to Thee,
   For Thou wilt never cast us out!
 Tho' shadows around us lie,
   Oh, Thou dost quell each fear and doubt!
 Thy mercy endureth still,
   Thou art our only hope and stay;
 Oh, keep us unto the end,
   And lead us Heavenward, day by day!

Thy Will be Done!

2 Teach us to humbly bend
  To all Thy love shall send;
  Keep us unto the end,—
    Thy will be done!
  Thy purpose who may know?
  Our hearts would fonder grow;
  In Heaven, and earth below,—
    Thy will be done!

Lead us Not.

Thine is the Kingdom.

Forever and Ever.

Almost in Sight.

2 Lo! our Father's at the helm;
   We fear nor storm nor wreck!—
Tho' the seas may overwhelm
   And sweep our vessel's deck!
Yes, we're sailing to the shore,
   And land's almost in sight!
In that Home forevermore,
   We'll anchor with delight!
Cho.—Sailing Homeward, &c.

2 All ye nations, bow before Him,
   He is God forevermore!
   With the Father now He reigneth,
   Heaven and earth His name,
   His holy name adore,
   Heaven and earth His name adore.
SOLO. { He hath opened to His people
         Glory's gates eternally!
         Christ is risen! Christ is risen!
         Spread the news from sea to sea.
CHO.—Shout Hosanna! He is victor, &c.

3 Come, ye ransomed, to His Temple,
   Sound His triumph to the skies!
   Come, ye faithful, ye repentant,
   With the risen Lord,
   The risen Lord arise,
   With your risen Lord arise.
SOLO. { See we now our souls' redemption,
         Jesus died and rose again,
         Christ is risen! Christ is risen!
         Life of all believing men.
CHO.—Shout Hosanna! He is victor, &c.

3. Tell the sweet and wondrous story,
   How the Son of God on high
   Left His home of peace and glory,
   In the realms beyond the sky!—Cho.

4. Sing of how He came to mortals
   Through His love and kindliness!—
   How He opened Heaven's bright portals,
   All His children here to bless!—Cho.

List our merry Carol!

CHRISTMAS CAROL.

2 See the star is beaming
　In the radiant East!
　And the song of glory
　　Nevermore hath ceased.
"Banish all unkindness;
　Be of gentle will!"
Angels ever near us
　Carol to us still.—Cho.

3 Joyful, joyful tidings
　Break upon the earth!
　Sing the Saviour's glory—
　　Tell his wondrous worth!
Every hill and valley
　Clad in pure white snow,
Breathes a merry carol,
　Echoed sweet and low.—Cho.

O, Lovely Star!

CHRISTMAS CAROL.

1. O, love-ly star that shone so bright, While Shepherds watched their flocks by night, To lead the wise men on their way, Where Christ our Lord and Sa-viour lay!
2. O, star that shone in brightness there, A-bove the Babe so sweet and fair. A-gain you beam a-bove the earth, And tell the Saviour's end-less worth!

CHORUS.
Hark! Hark! the cho-rus sounding still, From snowy vale and dis-tant hill! The An-gels breathe to earth a-gain, Peace on Earth, good will to men. Good will to men.

3.
O, Lovely Star! each cloud of gloom
Your beaming rays of joy illume!
And all our sorrow dies away,
When you have brought our Christmas day!
  Cho.—Hark! hark!

4.
Hosanna! to the Lord our King!
In cheerful voices we will sing;
Good angels answer us again:
Peace! Peace! on earth, good will to men.
  Cho.—Hark! hark!

2 Christ is born! Christ is born!
　　Wake the snow-clad hills and plains,
　Christ is born! Christ is born!
　　Lo! for evermore He reigns!
　　Earth seems clad in brightest beams,
　　E'en the sea more tranquil seems;
　　Every heart with gladness teems,
　　　Singing, Christ is born!

3 Christ is born! Christ is born!
　　Shout to heaven the hallowed strain,
　Christ is born! Christ is born!
　　Angels echo back again!
　　All the earth before Him bow,
　　Bright and fair be every brow!
　　Banish all unkindness now,
　　　Singing, "Christ is born!"

2 Oh, the loving smiles we share,
   Meeting round the Christmas tree!
Kindly hearts are everywhere,
   Meeting round the Christmas tree!
Blessed fruit it bears, we know,
Peace and Love for all below;
And it speaks of Bethlehem's Star,
Shining o'er the hills afar!—Cho.

3 Happy comrades, here we throng,
   Meeting round the Christmas tree;
Once again we swell the song,
   Meeting round the Christmas tree.
Ever green its branches grow
Mid the dreary frost and snow.
May our hearts, with mem'ries dear,
Keep their Christmas all the year!—Cho.

Christmas Bells!
CHRISTMAS CAROL.

1. Christ-mas bells are gai-ly ring-ing, Sing-ing, ring-ing on the air;
Sweet the mes-sage they are bring-ing, Chim-ing, rhym-ing ev-ery-where.
"Peace," they ut-ter, "Love and Glad-ness, Bless the heart up-on this morn!"
"Ban-ish ev-ery care and sad-ness, Christ our Lord to-day was born."

CHORUS. *ff*
Ringing, singing, chiming, rhyming, Christmas bells, how fair are they; Loud-ly swell-ing, fond-ly tell-ing Of the Sav-iour born to-day, Of the Sav-iour born to-day!

2 Living voices join their chorus,
　Singing, ringing loud and high;
Joyfully the angels o'er us
　Waft to earth their glad reply.
"Love," they echo, "Love unending
　Crown your hearts upon this morn,
For the Lord, to earth descending,
　On this blessed day was born!"

3 Christmas bells, so gaily ringing,
　Singing, ringing glad and free,
Peace and Good-will ever bringing,
　Wrap the world in melody!
Joy increasing, love and glory
　Unto every heart forlorn:
This your sweet and gentle story
　On the day that Christ was born!

Entered, according to Act of Congress, A. D. 1872, by H. MILLARD, in the Office of the Librarian of Congress at Washington

In the By-and-By.

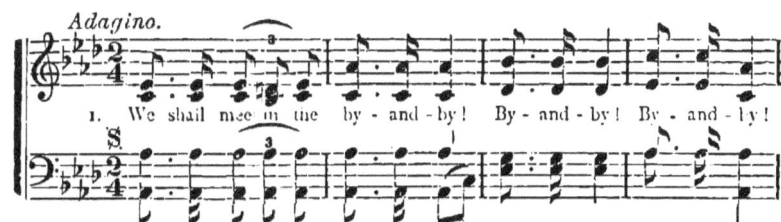

2.
We shall meet in the by-and-by!
By-and-by! By-and-by!
We shall meet in the by-and-by,
So wipe away every tear!
In our Father's mansions fair,
Angel hands will soothe our care:
O the love beyond compare,
Up in that home so dear!
We shall meet, &c.

3.
We shall meet in the by-and-by!
By-and-by! By-and-by!
We shall meet in the by-and-by!
Our journey will soon be done.
Here we wait a little while,
Where the toils of sin beguile,
Then we'll see the Saviour's smile,
After our victory's won!
We shall meet, &c.

Entered, according to Act of Congress, A. D. 1872, by H. MILLARD, in the Office of the Librarian of Congress at Washington.

Beautiful Mansions!

2 Beautiful mansions of the good!
　Lovingest arms will clasp us there!
　Beautiful mansions! beautiful mansions!
　Free from all sorrow and care!
　Honor and truth our motto shall be,
　Marching along, sweet Home, to thee,
　Stepping to sweetest melody,—
　　Nearing the land so fair!
Cho.—Beautiful mansions, &c.

3 Beautiful mansions of the true!
　Happiest land of perfect day!
　Beautiful mansions! beautiful mansions!
　Beaming in one endless May!
　Follow we on till life shall end,
　Jesus our Captain and our Friend;
　Comfort and succor he will send,
　　Lest we should go astray!
Cho.—Beautiful mansions, &c.

Entered according to Act of Congress, A.D. 1872, by H. MILLARD, in the office of the Librarian of Congress at Washington.

Work in God's Vineyard.

Moderato.

1. Work in God's vineyard! the work-ers are few! Lo! there is something for each one to do. No hand so weak that its por-tion of toil Fall-eth un-seen on the boun-ti-ful soil.
2. Work in God's vineyard! oh, scat-ter the seed; Help the af-flict-ed who wan-der in need. Tell of the Sa-viour who bids them to come; Glad-den the hearts that to glad-ness are dumb.

CHORUS.

Work in God's vineyard! oh, work with a will! Mil-lions a-round us are hun-ger-ing still.
Work in God's vineyard! He bids thee straightway; Work for the Mas-ter, while yet it is day!

Work then, for quickly the night cometh on; Work till the Master proclaimeth, 'Well done!'
Work with thy heart and thy soul and thy might, Work till the beau-ti-ful Land is in sight!

Father, keep us thro' the day.

(MORNING HYMN.)

2 Shield us with Thy loving care;
Oh, receive our morning prayer;
Teach us, Lord, to do Thy will,
Be our guide and shepherd still.
Thou who dost the ravens feed,
Thou dost know each earthly need;
Snares and pitfalls mark our way:
Father, keep us thro' the day!

Ask, and it Shall be given.

1. Ask and it shall be giv-en, Thy Lord hath promised thee; Whate'er thy spir-it needeth, What-e'er thy want may be. With hum-ble hearts and grate-ful, Oh, kneel before His throne! For every heart's af-flictions To Him, to Him are known. Thy Fa-ther up in Heav-en, Thy Fa-ther up in Heav-en, Ask, and it shall be giv-en! Ask, and it shall be giv-en! Ask! ask! ask, and it shall be giv'n!

2. His bread of joy and comfort Shall bid thy hunger cease; His wine, of Life un-dy-ing, Shall bring thee endless peace. So eve-ry-one that ask-eth, He giveth in de-light; Come all ye poor and needy, And trust His loving might. Thy

Three Golden Words.

2 There is a word so fond and sweet,
   To human hearts so dear;
   Blest refuge for our weary feet,
   When days are dark and drear.
   We seek in vain its joys to find,
   Tho' far and wide we roam;
   Oh, blessings on its inmates kind;
   Sweet blessings on our Home!
   Our ever-loving Home!

3 There is a word of purest joy
   Combining Home and Love;
   Sweet Land where nothing may annoy,—
   Dear Land of Light above!
   Oh, refuge for the weary soul!
   Oh, balm to wand'rers given!
   Thank God, while storms around us roll,
   For Love and Home and Heaven!
   Our Love and Home and Heaven!

2 The year has brought its gifts to all,
And passed away beyond recall;
But here we welcome Teachers kind,
And loving comrades here we find.
We thank our Father for His care,
And all the gladness that we share;
We thank Him for His glorious earth,
And shout aloud His wondrous worth.

3 Then Teachers, comrades, fond and dear,
Oh, may we meet another year,
And join our voices, glad as now,
With light and joy upon each brow.
A welcome sweet to all our friends;
With grateful hearts for what God sends,
Oh, may we fondly gathering,
Oft meet again His praise to sing!

2 Thou art strong, but we are weak,
    Father, lift us up!
   To all hearts Thy comfort speak,
    Father, lift us up!
   Lest we fail to do Thy will,
   Be our guide and shepherd still;
   From the paths of earthly ill,
    Father, lift us up!

3 Nearer to Thee, day by day,
    Father, lift us up!
   To the bright and Heav'nly way,
    Father, lift us up!
   From the burdens that we share,
   From the weariness of care,
   From the darkness of despair,
    Father, lift us up!

2 Joys that have departed
  We will share once more;
  Hopes that here have withered,
  Heav'n will soon restore.
  Every precious promise
    God will there fulfill;
  When we cross the river,
    At His blessed will!

3 All our cares and sorrows
  We shall leave on earth;
  Only joy and gladness
  In that land have birth.
  Soon will come the message
    That will bear us o'er;
  Soon we'll meet our dear ones,
    On the golden shore!

Little Ones who Walk in Light.

Moderato con espressione.

1. Oh, how pleasant, in Life's morning, To re-vere the Saviour's name! Like sweet flow'rs the earth a-dorning, Lips that His dear love proclaim! For the world with all its beau-ty, Ne'er can show so fair a sight, As young hearts attuned to du-ty, Lit-tle

CHORUS.

ones who walk in light! Sweeter than the sweetest blossom; Fairer than the stars of night; Dear un-to the Saviour's bo-som, Lit-tle ones who walk in Light!

2 Oh, the Saviour, kind and loving,
 Bade the children to Him come,—
Those who would deny reproving;
 Sweetest lesson while we roam.
Even now He looks in glory,
 On His dear ones, with delight!
Still we sing His blessed story,—
 Little ones who walk in Light!

3 Let us then, His praises singing,
 Gather in His Holy place;
To His precepts fondly clinging,—
 Sunshine in each youthful face.
Oh, the world, with all its beauty,
 Ne'er can show so fair a sight,
As young hearts attuned to duty,—
 Little ones who walk in Light!

Seek, and ye Shall Find.

Faith.

2 Without Thy hand, oh, Father,
   We soon should faint and fail;
Without Thy love and goodness,
   What would our strength avail?
Oh, keep us ever near Thee;
   Thy word our armor be;
Thy love be our protection,
   Along Life's tossing sea.
Forever keep us faithful,
   Still faithful unto Thee!

Charity.

2 Teach us Lord its pleasant duties,
  Keep us in its gentle ways;
  May its kindly whispers reach us
  In our bright and youthful days.
  Doing acts of loving kindness
  That we more resemble Thee,—
  Help us, Lord, to love forever,
  Charity, sweet Charity!

Blessed are They that Mourn.

2 No joys are lasting here,
   No path is always bright;
No heart's unknown to fear,
   To all must fall the night.
Sad hearts by sorrow torn,
   Thy Saviour, this hath said:
Blessed are they that mourn,
   They shall be comforted!
Blessed are they that mourn,
   They shall be comforted!

Blessed are The Meek.

87

Blessed are They that Hunger.

Blessed are the Merciful.

Moderato con espressione.
SOLO, (*or in Unison.*)

1. Bless-ed are the mer - ciful, For mercy shall be theirs; He, to whom we

humbly plead, Will hear our fervent prayers. God in pi - ty looks on all His

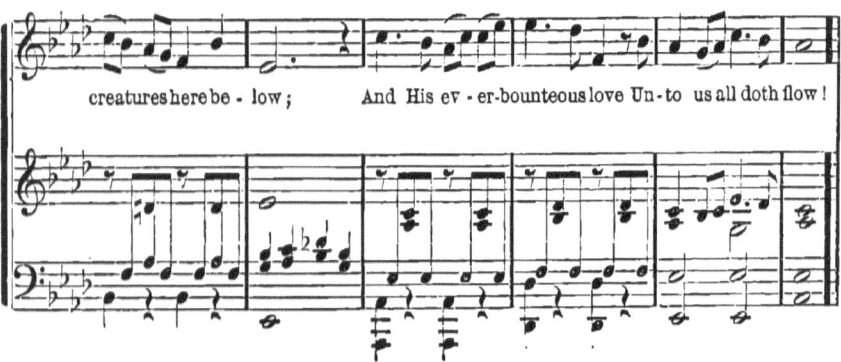

creatures here be - low; And His ev - er-bounteous love Un-to us all doth flow!

2 Blessed are the merciful,
　Oh, scatter words of cheer;
E'en a smile, in kindness given,
　Some gloomy sky may clear.
As the Lord doth mercy show
　Unto each erring one,
So, withhold no kindly act,
　While here thy days are run!
CHORUS.—Blessed are the merciful, &c.

Blessed are the Peacemakers.

2 Blessed are the peacemakers,—
   The children of their God!
Breathing sweetest incense round,
   Like daisies from the sod.
Calming every angry storm
   That rages in the soul;
Mirroring bright Heav'n above,
   While Time shall onward roll.
CHORUS.—Blessed are the peacemakers, &c.

Blessed are they that are Persecuted.

Chants.

No. 1.   **Psalm XXIII.**

1. The Lord is my shepherd, I | shall | not | want; | He maketh me to lie down in green pastures; He leadeth me be- | side | the | still — | waters.
2. He re- - - - - - | storeth my | soul; | He leadeth me in the paths of righteousness... | for | His | name's— | sake.
3. Yea, tho' I walk thro' the valley of the............ | shadow of | death; | I will............ | fear | no | e- - | vil.
4. For..................... | Thou art | with me; | Thy rod and Thy | staff | they | com-fort | me.
5. Thou preparest a table before me in the......... | presence of mine | enemies; | Thou anointest my head with oil;.. | my | cup | run-neth | over.
6. Surely goodness and mercy shall follow me all the .. | days of my | life; | And I will dwell in the......... | house of the | Lord for | ever.
                                                                                               A- | men

No. 2.   **St. Luke 1: 68-71.**

1. Blessed be the Lord...... | God of | Israel; | For He hath visited | and re- | deemed His | people;
2. And hath raised up a mighty sal- - - - | va-tion | for us: | In the house...... | of His | ser-vant | David;
3. As He spake by the mouth of His,............... | ho-ly | Prophets, | Which have been .. | since the | world be- | gan;
4. That we should be saved.. | from our | enemies, | And from the...... | hand of | all that | hate us.
Glory be to the Father, and to the Son, And .... to the Ho-ly Ghost;
As it was in the beginning, is now, and........... | ev-er | shall be: | World............ | with-out | end. A- | men.

No. 3.   **Psalm XXVI.**

1. I will wash my..... | hands in | innocency, | O Lord, and.. | so will I | go to Thine | altar.
2. That I may show the | voice of thanks- | giving; | And will tell of | all Thy | won-drous | works.
3. Lord, I have lov'd the habitation .... | of Thy | house; | And the place | where Thine | hon-or | dwelleth.
5. I will walk innocently, O de- - - | liv-er | me; | And be...... | mer-ci- | ful un- | to me.
6. I will praise the Lord in the............ | con-gre- | gations; | There........ | will I | bless the | Lord.
                                                                                               A- | men.

Chants.

Venite, Exultemus Domino.

No. 4.   MORNING SERVICE.

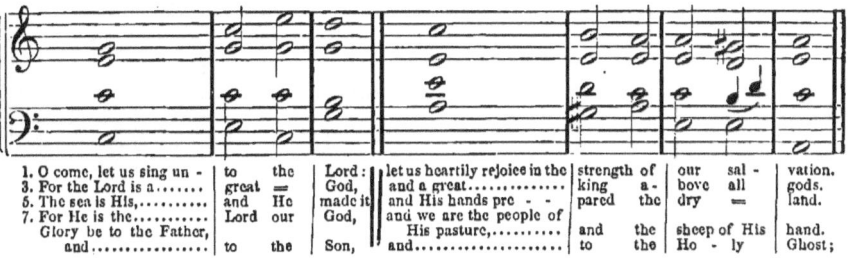

1. O come, let us sing un- | to the | Lord : | let us heartily rejoice in the | strength of | our sal- | vation.
3. For the Lord is a...... | great | God, | and a great............... | king a- | bove all | gods.
5. The sea is His,.......... | and | He | made it | and His hands pre- - | pared the | dry | land.
7. For He is the............ | Lord | our | God, | and we are the people of
Glory be to the Father, | | | | His pasture,.......... | and the | sheep of His | hand.
and................. | to | the | Son, | and..................... | to the | Ho - ly | Ghost;

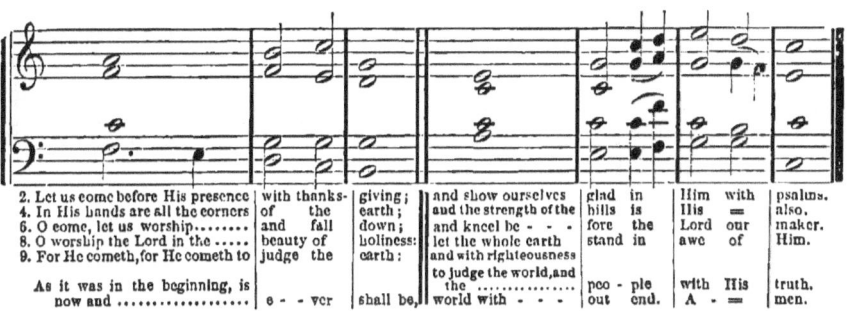

2. Let us come before His presence | with thanks- | giving; | and show ourselves | glad in | Him with | psalms.
4. In His hands are all the corners | of the | earth; | and the strength of the | hills is | His | also.
6. O come, let us worship........ | and fall | down; | and kneel be- - - | fore the | Lord our | maker.
8. O worship the Lord in the..... | beauty of | holiness: | let the whole earth | stand in | awe of | Him.
9. For He cometh, for He cometh to | judge the | earth : | and with righteousness
to judge the world, and
As it was in the beginning, is | | | the .... | peo - ple | with His | truth.
now and .... | e - - ver | shall be, | world with - - - | out end. | A - | men.

Oppure.

9. For He com-eth, for He com-eth to judge the

earth: And with right-eousness to judge the world, and the peo-ple with His truth.

Chants.

Jubilate Deo.

No. 5. MORNING SERVICE, AFTER SECOND LESSON.

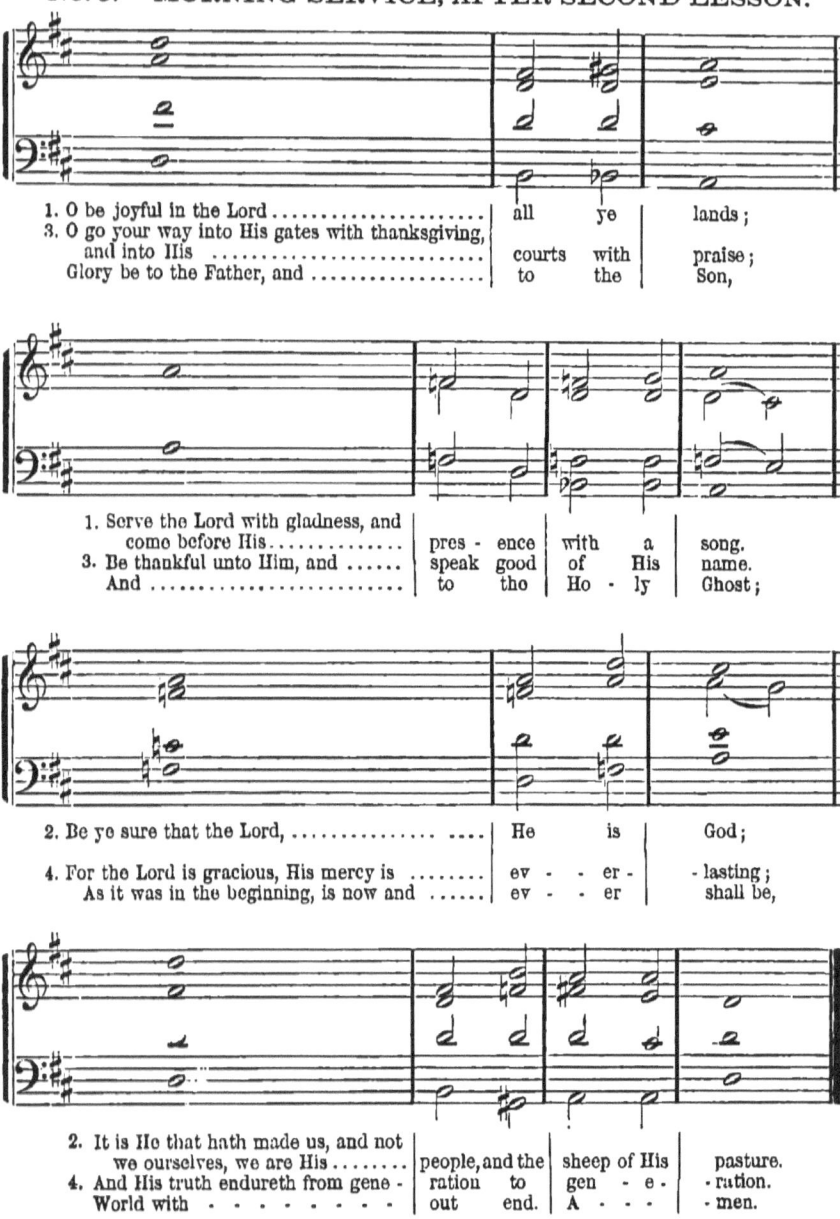

Chants.
Cantate Domino.
No. 7. EVENING SERVICE, AFTER FIRST LESSON.

Chants.

Bonum est Confiteri.

No. 8. EVENING SERVICE, AFTER FIRST LESSON.

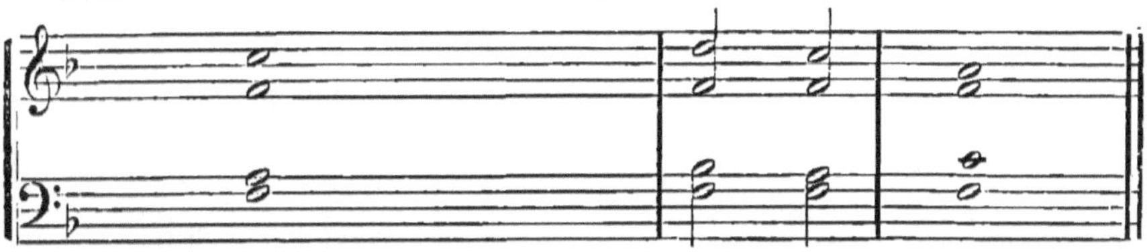

1. It is a good thing to give thanks un - - - | to the | Lord,
3. Upon an instrument of ten strings, and up - | on the | lute;
Glory be to the Father, and .... | to the | Son,

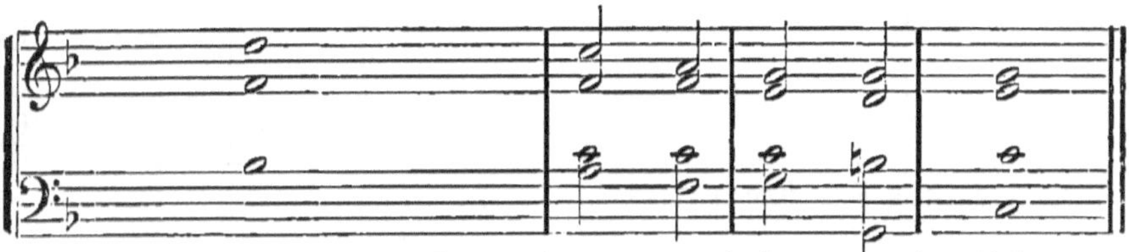

1. and to sing praises unto Thy .... | name, = | O most | highest.
3. upon a loud instrument.......... | and up - | on the | harp.
and .... | to the | Ho - - ly | Ghost;

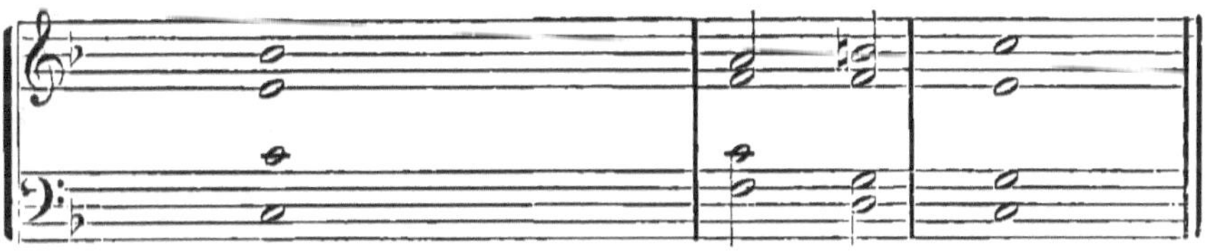

2. To tell of Thy loving kindness............. | early in the | morning;
4. For thou, Lord, hast made me glad .... | through Thy | works;
As it was in the beginning, is now and ..... | ev - - er | shall be,

2. and of Thy truth................ | in the | night = | season.
4. and I will rejoice in giving praise for the ope - - - - | ra - - tion | of Thy | hands.
world with - - - - - - - - | out end. | A - - — | men.

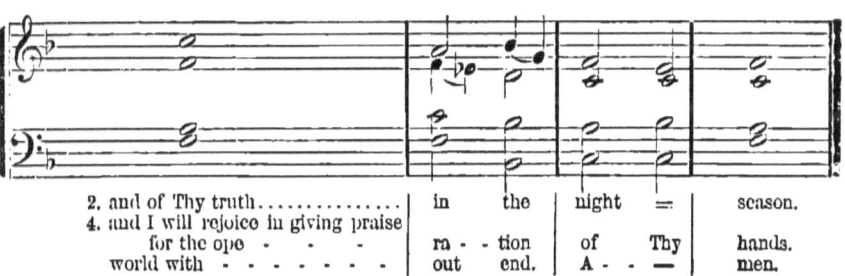

Chants.

Deus Misereatur.

No. 9. EVENING SERVICE, AFTER SECOND LESSON.

1. God be merciful unto .... | us, and | bless us :
3. Let the people .... | praise thee, O | God :
5. Let the people .... | praise thee, O | God :
   Glory be to the Father, and .... | to the | Son,

1 and show us the light of His countenance, and be .... | mer - ci - | ful un - | to us.
3 yea, let .... | all the | peo - ple | praise Thee.
5 yea, let .... | all the | peo - ple | praise Thee.
  and .... | to the | Ho - ly | Ghost;

2. That thy way may be .... | known upon | earth :
4. O let the nations re - - - - - - | joice and be | glad :
6. Then shall the earth bring .... | forth her | increase :
7. God .... | shall = | bless us :
   As it was in the beginning, is now and ..... | ev - - er | shall be,

2 Thy saving .... | health a - | mong all | nations.
4 for Thou shalt judge the folk righteously, and govern the .... | na - tions | up - on | earth :
6 and God, even our own .... | God, shall | give us His | blessing.
7 and all the ends of the .... | world shall | fear = | Him.
  world with - - - - - - - - | out | end. A - - — | men.

Chants.

Benedic, Anima Mea.

No. 10. EVENING SERVICE, AFTER SECOND LESSON.

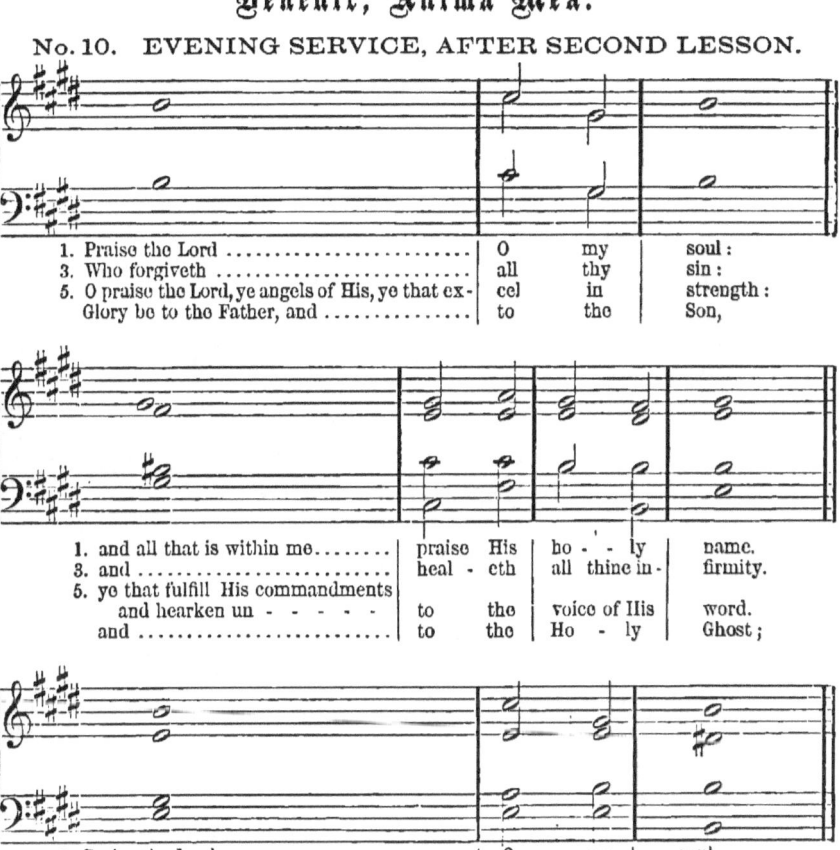

Concert Exercise
ON
THE LORD'S PRAYER.

In "Millard's Sunday School Chaplet."

Read Luke xi:1-13.

The Superintendent, after a few prefatory remarks on the origin and beauty of the LORD'S PRAYER, announces that illustrations will be made musically, of each phrase; and by recitations, of each word. He then announces—

Our Father which art in Heaven.

SUPT.—*Our.*

SCHOOL.—(*reciting slowly and distinctly*)—Doubtless thou art *our* Father, though Abraham be ignorant of us, and Israel acknowledge us not; thou, O Lord, art *our* Father; *our* Redeemer, thy name is from everlasting.—ISAIAH lxiii. 16.

SUPT.—*Father.*

SCHOOL.—Like as a *Father* pitieth his children, so the Lord pitieth them that fear him.—Ps. ciii. 13.

SUPT.—*Which art.*

SCHOOL.—And God saith unto Moses, *I am that I am;* and he said, thus shalt thou say unto the children of Israel, *I am* hath sent me unto you.—Ex. iii. 14.

SUPT.—*In heaven.*

SCHOOL.—Be not rash with thy mouth, and let not thine heart be hasty to utter anything before God, *for God is in Heaven* and thou upon earth, therefore let thy words be few.—(ECCL. v. 2.) Know therefore this day, and consider it in thine heart, that the Lord he is God *in Heaven* above and upon the earth beneath; there is none else.—DEUT. iv. 39.

Sing p. 33, "Our Father," etc.
(Aided by the Choir of the Church, if possible.)

Hallowed be thy name.

SUPT.—*Hallowed be.*

SCHOOL.—Neither shall ye profane my holy name; but I will *be hallowed* among the children of Israel; I am the Lord which *hallow* you.—LEV. xxii. 32.

SUPT.—*Thy.*

SCHOOL.—Not unto us, O Lord, not unto us, but unto *thy* name give glory, for *thy* mercy, and for *thy* truth's sake.—Ps. cxv. 1.

SUPT.—*Name.*

SCHOOL.—Thy *name*, O Lord, endureth for ever, and thy memorial, O Lord, throughout all generations.—(Ps. cxxxv. 13.) Stand up and bless the Lord your God for ever and ever, and blessed be thy glorious *name*, which is exalted above all blessing and praise.—(NEH. ix. 5.)—That thou mayest fear this glorious and fearful *name*, the Lord thy God.—DEUT. xxviii. 58.

Sing p. 34, "Hallowed be thy name."

Thy kingdom come.

SUPT.—*Thy.*

SCHOOL.—*Thy* kingdom is an everlasting kingdom: and *thy* dominion endureth throughout all generations.—Ps. cxlv. 13.

SUPT.—*Kingdom.*

SCHOOL.—For the *kingdom* is the Lord's; and he is governor among the nations.—(Ps. xxii. 28)—They shall speak of the glory of thy *kingdom* and talk of thy power.—(Ps. cxlv. 11.)—To make known to the sons of men his mighty acts, and the glorious majesty of his *kingdom*.—Ps. cxlv. 12.

SUPT.—*Come.*

SCHOOL.—And when he was demanded of the Pharisees, when the kingdom of God should *come*, he answered them and said, The kingdom of God *cometh* not with observation.—(LUKE xvii. 20.)—Neither shall they say, Lo here! or, lo there! for, behold, the *kingdom* of God is within you.—LUKE xvii. 21.

Sing p. 35, "Thy kingdom come."
(Solo and Chorus, if possible.)

Thy will be done in earth as it is in heaven.

SUPT.—*Thy.*

SCHOOL.—Nevertheless *not my* will but *thine* be done —LUKE xxii. 42.

SUPT.—*Will.*

SCHOOL.—Even so it is not the *will* of your Father that one of these little ones should perish.—(MATT. xviii. 14.) And this is the Father's *will* which sent me, that of all which he has given me I should lose nothing, but should raise it up again at the last day.—(JOHN vi. 39.) And this is the *will* of him which sent me, that every one which seeth the son and believeth on him may have everlasting life, and I will raise him up at the last day.—JOHN vi. 40.

SUPT.—*Be done.*

SCHOOL.—If ye abide in me, and my words abide in you, ye shall ask what ye will and it *shall be done* unto you.—(JOHN xv. 7.) For he spake and it *was done*, he commanded and it stood fast.—Ps. xxxiii. 9.

SUPT.—*In earth.*

SCHOOL.—And blessed be his glorious name forever; and let the whole *earth* be filled with his glory.—(Ps. lxxi. 19.)—All the *earth* shall worship thee, and shall sing unto thee.—(Ps. lxvi. 4.

SUPT.—*As it is.*

SCHOOL.—He doeth *according to his will* in the army of heaven, and among the inhabitants of earth.—DAN. iv. 35.

SUPT.—*In heaven.*

SCHOOL.—Forever, O Lord, thy word is settled *in heaven.*—Ps. cxii. 89.

Sing p. 36, "Thy will be done."

Give us this day our daily bread.

SUPT.—*Give.*

SCHOOL.—Ask and it shall be *given* you.—Matt. vii. 7.

SUPT.—*Us.*

SCHOOL.—Ask of God who *giveth* to all men liberally.—(JAS. i. 5.—For *every* one that asketh receiveth.—Matt. vii. 8.

SUPT.—*This day.*

SCHOOL.—And it shall come to pass that *before they call* I will answer, and *while they are yet speaking* I will hear.—ISAIAH xv. 24.

SUPT.—*Our.*

SCHOOL.—*They that seek* the Lord shall not want any good thing.—Ps. xxxiv. 10.

SUPT.—*Daily.*

SCHOOL.—*Take no thought* for your life, what ye shall eat; neither for the body what ye shall put on.—LUKE xii. 22.

SUPT.—*Bread.*

SCHOOL.—*Casting all* your care on *him*, for he careth for you. 1 Pet. v. 7.)—Consider the ravens, for they neither sow nor reap, which neither have store-house nor barn; and God *feedeth* them; how much more are ye better than the fowls.—LUKE xii. 24.—I will *feed* my flock, saith the Lord God.—(EZEK. xxxiv. 15. —The Lord is my Shepherd, *I shall not want.*—Ps. xxiii. L.

Sing p. 37, "Give us this day."

And forgive us our trespasses.

SUPT.—*And forgive.*

SCHOOL.—Who can *forgive* sins but God only? MARK ii. 7.

SUPT.—*Us.*

SCHOOL.—If *we* say that *we* have no sin we deceive ourselves and the truth is not is *us*. 1 JOHN i. 18.

SUPT.—*Our.*

SCHOOL.—If we confess *our* sins, he is faithful and just to forgive us *our* sins and to cleanse us from all unrighteousness. 1 JOHN i. 9.

SUPT.—*Trespasses.*

SCHOOL.—If we say we have not *sinned* we make him a liar, and his word is not in us. 1 JOHN i. 10.

Sing p. 38, "Forgive us our trespasses."

As we forgive those who trespass against us.

SUPT.—*As we.*

SCHOOL.—For if *ye* forgive men their trespasses, your heavenly father will also forgive you.—MATT. vi. 14.—But if *ye* forgive not men their *trespasses*, neither will your father forgive your *trespasses.*—MATT. vi. 15.

SUPT.—*Forgive.*

SCHOOL.—Then came Peter to him and said, Lord, how oft shall my brother sin against me, and I *forgive* him? till seven times?—MATT. xviii. 21.—Jesus saith unto him, I say not unto thee until seven times, but until seventy times seven.—MATT. xviii. 22.

SUPT.—*Those who.*

SCHOOL.—Shouldst not *thou* also have had compassion on *thy fellow servant*, even as I had pity on thee? MATT. xviii. 33.

SUPT.—*Trespass against us.*

SCHOOL.—If thy *brother trespass against thee*, rebuke him and if he repent, forgive him.—LUKE xvii. ?

Sing p. 39 "As we forgive," etc.

And lead us not into temptation.

SUPT.—*And lead.*

SCHOOL.—If I take the wings of the morning, and dwell in the uttermost parts of the sea; even there shall thy hand lead me, and thy right hand shall hold me.—(Ps. cxxxix. 9, 10.)—O send out thy light and thy truth; let them *lead* me, let them bring me unto thy holy will and to thy tabernacles.—(Ps. xliii. 3.

SUPT.—*Us.*

SCHOOL.—Even *us*, whom he hath called, not of the Jews only but 'so of the gentiles.—ROM. ix. 24.

SUPT.—*Not.*

SCHOOL.—Let no man say when he is tempted, I am tempted of God; for God can *not* be tempted of evil, *neither* tempteth he any man.—JAS. i. 13.

SUPT.—*Into temptation.*

SCHOOL.—Because thou hast kept the word of my patience, I also will keep thee from the hour of *temptation* which shall come upon all the world, to try them that dwelt upon the earth.—(REV. iii. 10.) There hath no *temptation* taken you but such as is common to man; but God is faithful, who will not suffer you to be tempted above that ye are able; but will with the *temptation* also make a way of escape that ye may be able to bear it.—(1 COR. x. 13.)—Blessed is the man that endureth *temptation.*—JAS. i. 12.

Sing p. 40, "Lead us not."
(Solo, Soprano if possible.)

But deliver us from evil.

SUPT.—*But deliver.*

SCHOOL.—Grace be to you, and peace, from our Lord Jesus Christ, who gave himself for our sins, that he might *deliver* us from this present evil world.—GAL. i. 3, 4.

SUPT.—*Us.*

SCHOOL.—The Lord made not this covenant with our fathers, but with *us*, even *us*, who are all of us here alive this day.— DEUT. v. 3.

SUPT.—*From evil.*

SCHOOL.—By the fear of the Lord men depart *from evil.*— (PROV. xvi. 6.)—But the Lord is faithful, who shall stablish you and keep you from evil.—2 THESS. iii. 3.

Sing p. 41, "Deliver us from evil."

For thine is the kingdom.

SUPT.—*For thine.*

SCHOOL.—*Thine*, O Lord, is the greatness, and the power, and the glory, and the victory, and the majesty; for all that is in the heaven and in the earth is *thine; thine* is the kingdom, O Lord, and thou art exalted as head above all.—(1 CHRON. xxix. 11.)—The heavens are *thine*, the earth also is thine; as for the world and the fullness thereof, thou hast founded them. —Ps. lxxxix. 11.

SUPT.—*Is the kingdom.*

SCHOOL.—And the *kingdom* and dominion, and the greatness of the *kingdom* under the whole heaven, shall be given to the people of the saints of the Most High, whose *kingdom* is an everlasting *kingdom*, and all dominions shall serve and obey him.—DAN. vii. 27.

Sing p. 42, "Thine is the kingdom."

And the power, and the glory forever. Amen.

SUPT.—*And the power.*

SCHOOL.—And every creature which is in heaven and on the earth, and under the earth, and such as are in the sea, and all that are in them, heard I saying, Blessing, and honour, and glory, and *power*, be unto him that sitteth upon the throne, and unto the lamb, forever and ever.—(REV. v. 13.) And after these things I heard a great voice of much people in heaven, saying, Alleluia; salvation, and glory, and honour, and *power*, unto the Lord our God.—REV. xix. 1.

SUPT.—*And the glory.*

SCHOOL.—Lift up your heads, O ye gates, even lift them up, ye everlasting doors; and the King of *glory* shall come in.— (Ps. xxiv. 9.) Who is this King of *glory*? The Lord of hosts, he is the King of *glory.*—Ps. xxiv. 10.

SUPT.—*Forever.*

SCHOOL.—For a *thousand years* in thy sight are but as yesterday when it is past and as a watch in the night.—(Ps. xc 4.) But thou art the same, and thy years shall have no end.— (Ps. cii. 27.) Thy years are throughout all generations.—Ps. cii. 24.

Sing p. 43, "Forever and ever."

The Beatitudes:

A CONCERT EXERCISE,

By J. G. SNELLING.

SUPT.—What is the meaning of the word Beatitude?

SCHOOL.—Happiness.

SUPT.—Who are the truly happy?

SCHOOL.—Whoso trusteth in the Lord, happy is he.—Prov. 16 : 20.

SUPT.—What is the first Beatitude?

TEACHER.—**Blessed are the poor in spirit: for theirs is the kingdom of heaven.**

SUPT.—What does the Bible say of the poor in spirit?

Responsive Readings.

BOYS.

1. The Lord is nigh unto them that are of a broken heart; and saveth such as be of a contrite spirit. Ps. 34: 18.

2. Better is it to be of an humble spirit with the lowly, than to divide the spoil with the proud.—Prov. 16: 19.

3. For thus saith the high and lofty One that inhabiteth eternity, whose name is Holy; I dwell in the high and holy place, with him also that is of a contrite and humble spirit, to revive the spirit of the humble, and to revive the heart of the contrite ones. Isa. 57: 15.

4. Humble yourselves in the sight of the Lord, and he shall lift you up.—James 4: 10.

GIRLS.

1. The sacrifices of God are a broken spirit: a broken and a contrite heart, O God, thou wilt not despise.—Ps. 51: 17.

2. A man's pride shall bring him low: but honor shall uphold the humble in spirit.—Prov. 29: 23.

3. For all those things hath mine hands made, and all those things have been, saith the Lord: but to this man will I look, even to him that is poor and of a contrite spirit, and trembleth at my word.—Isa. 66: 2.

4. And the Publican, standing afar off, would not lift so much as his eyes unto heaven, but smote upon his breast, saying, God be merciful to me a sinner.

I tell you, this man went down to his house justified rather than the other: for every one that exalteth himself shall be abased; and he that humbleth himself shall be exalted.—Luke 18: 13 & 14.

Sing p. 85.

SUPT.—What is the second Beatitude?

TEACHER.—**Blessed are they that mourn: for they shall be comforted.**

SUPT.—What comfort may the mourner find in God's Word?

BOYS.

1. He will swallow up death in victory; and the Lord God will wipe away tears from off all faces; and the rebuke of the people shall he take away from off all the earth; for the Lord hath spoken it.—Isa. 25: 8.

2. The spirit of the Lord God is upon me; because the Lord hath anointed me to preach good tidings unto the meek; he hath sent me to bind up the broken hearted, to proclaim liberty to the captives, and the opening of the prison to them that are bound.

To proclaim the acceptable year of the Lord, and the day of vengeance of our God; to comfort all that mourn; to appoint unto them that mourn in Zion, to give unto them beauty for ashes, the oil of joy for mourning, the garment of praise for the spirit of heaviness; that they might be called trees of righteousness, the planting of the Lord, that he might be glorified.—Isa. 61 : 1–3.

GIRLS.

1. Therefore, the redeemed of the Lord shall return, and come with singing unto Zion; and everlasting joy shall be upon their head: they shall obtain gladness and joy; and sorrow and mourning shall flee away.—Isa. 51: 11.

2. Blessed be God, even the Father of our Lord Jesus Christ, the Father of mercies, and the God of all comfort;

Who comforteth us in all our tribulation, that we may be able to comfort them which are in any trouble, by the comfort wherewith we ourselves are comforted of God.

For as the sufferings of Christ abound in us, so our consolation also aboundeth in Christ.—II Cor 3: 4 & 5.

BOYS.

3. And in that day thou shalt say, O Lord, I will praise thee; though thou wast angry with me, thine anger is turned away, and thou comfortedst me.—Isa. 12: 1.

4. For godly sorrow worketh repentance to salvation not to be repented of: but the sorrow of the world worketh death.—II Cor. 7: 10.

GIRLS.

3. They that sow in tears shall reap in joy. He that goeth forth and weepeth, bearing precious seed, shall doubtless come again with rejoicing, bringing his sheaves with him.—Ps. 126: 5 & 6.

4. And he said unto me, these are they which came out of great tribulation, and have washed their robes, and made them white in the blood of the Lamb; and God shall wipe away all tears from their eyes.—Rev. 7: 14 & 17.

Sing p. 86.

SUPT.—What is the next Beatitude?

TEACHER.—Blessed are the meek: for they shall inherit the earth.

SUPT.—Will you give some Bible promises concerning the meek?

BOYS.

1. The meek shall eat and be satisfied: they shall praise the Lord that seek him: your heart shall live forever.—Ps. 22: 26.

2. For the Lord taketh pleasure in his people: he will beautify the meek with salvation.—Ps. 149: 4.

3. Who is a wise man and endued with knowledge among you? let him show out of a good conversation his works with meekness of wisdom.—James 3: 13.

4. But let it be the hidden man of the heart, in that which is not corruptible, even the ornament of a meek and quiet spirit, which is in the sight of God of great price.—I Peter 3: 4.

GIRLS.

1. The meek will he guide in judgment: and the meek will he teach his way.—Ps. 25: 9.

2. Seek ye the Lord, all ye meek of the earth, which have wrought his judgment; seek righteousness, seek meekness: it may be ye shall be hid in the day of the Lord's anger.

3. Put on, therefore, as the elect of God, holy and beloved, bowels of mercies, kindness, humbleness of mind, meekness.—Col. 3: 12.

4. Take my yoke upon you, and learn of me; for I am meek and lowly in heart: and ye shall find rest unto your souls.—Matt. 11: 29.

Sing p. 87.

SUPT.—What is the fourth Beatitude?

TEACHER.—Blessed are they which do hunger and thirst after righteousness: for they shall be filled.

SUPT.—What is said in the Word of God about spiritual hunger and thirst?

BOYS.

1. Ho, every one that thirsteth, come ye to the waters, and he that hath no money; come ye, buy, and eat; yea, come, buy wine and milk without money and without price. Wherefore do ye spend money for that which is not bread, and your labor for that which satisfieth not? hearken diligently unto me, and eat ye that which is good, and let your soul delight itself in fatness.—Isa. 55: 1 & 2.

2. For he satisfieth the longing soul, and filleth the hungry soul with goodness.—Ps. 107: 9.

3. They shall not hunger nor thirst; neither shall the heat nor sun smite them: for he that hath mercy on them shall lead them, even by the springs of water shall he guide them.—Isa. 49: 10.

4. I am the living bread which came down from heaven: if any man eat of this bread, he shall live forever: and the bread that I will give is my flesh, which I will give for the life of the world.—John 51.

GIRLS.

1. As the hart panteth after the water brooks, so panteth my soul after thee, O God. My soul thirsteth for God, for the living God: when shall I come and appear before God.—Ps. 42: 7 & 2.

2. O God, thou art my God; early will I seek thee, my soul thirsteth for thee, my flesh longeth for thee in a dry and thirsty land where no water is.—Ps. 63: 1.

3. Labor not for the meat which perisheth, but for that meat which endureth unto everlasting life, which the son of man shall give unto you; for him hath God the Father sealed.—John 6: 27.

4. But whosoever drinketh of the water that I shall give him shall never thirst; but the water that I shall give him shall be in him a well of water springing up into everlasting life.—John 4: 14.

Sing p. 88.

Supt.—What is the next Beatitude?

Teacher.—Blessed are the merciful: for they shall obtain mercy.

Supt.—Who are the merciful?

BOYS.

1. Blessed is he that considereth the poor: for the Lord will deliver him in time of trouble. The Lord will preserve him, and keep him alive; and he shall be blessed upon the earth.—Ps. 41: 1 & 2.

2. The merciful man doeth good to his own soul; but he that is cruel troubleth his own flesh.—Prov. 11: 17.

3. He that hath pity upon the poor lendeth unto the Lord; and that which he hath given will he pay him again.—Prov. 19: 17.

4. And be ye kind one to another, tender hearted, forgiving, one another, even as God for Christ's sake hath forgiven you.—Eph. 4: 32.

GIRLS.

1. A good man sheweth favor and lendeth: he will guide his affairs with discretion.
He hath dispersed, he hath given to the poor; his righteousness endureth forever; his horn shall be exalted with honor.—Ps. 112: 5 & 9.

2. He that despiseth his neighbor sinneth: but he that hath mercy on the poor, happy is he.—Prov. 14: 21.

3. He hath showed thee, O man, what is good; and what doth the Lord require of thee, but to do justly, and to love mercy, and to walk humbly with thy God?—Micah 6: 8.

4. But love your enemies, and do good, and lend, hoping for nothing again; and your reward shall be great, and ye shall be the children of the Highest: for he is kind unto the the unthankful and to the evil. Be ye therefore merciful, as your Father also is merciful.—Luke 6: 35 & 36.

Sing p. 89.

Supt.—What is the next Beatitude?

Teacher.—Blessed are the pure in heart: for they shall see God.

Supt.—What else do we find in the Bible about the pure hearted?

BOYS.

1. Who shall ascend into the hill of the Lord? or who shall stand in his holy place?—Ps. 24: 3.

2. Create in me a clean heart, O God; and renew a right spirit within me.—Ps. 51: 10.

3. Unto the pure all things are pure; but unto them that are defiled and unbelieving is nothing pure; but even their mind and conscience is defiled.—Titus 1: 15.

4. Let us draw near with a true heart in full assurance of faith, having our hearts sprinkled from an evil conscience, and our bodies washed with pure water.—Heb. 10: 22.

GIRLS.

1. He that hath clean hands and a pure heart; who hath not lifted up his soul unto vanity, nor sworn deceitfully. Ps. 24: 4.

2. He that loveth pureness of heart, for the grace of his lips the king shall be his friend.—Prov. 22: 11.

3. How much more shall the blood of Christ, who through the eternal Spirit offered himself without spot to God, purge your conscience from dead works to serve the living God.—Heb. 9: 14.

4. Seeing ye have purified your souls in obeying the truth through the Spirit unto unfeigned love of the brethren, see that ye love one another with a pure heart fervently.—I Pet. 1: 22.

Sing p. 90 & 91.

Supt.—What is the seventh Beatitude?

Teacher.—Blessed are the peacemakers: for they shall be called the children of God.

Supt.—What may we learn in the Scriptures of our duty to those around us?

BOYS.

1. I therefore, the prisoner of the Lord, beseech you, that ye walk worthy of the vocation wherewith ye are called,
With all lowliness and meekness, with long-suffering, forbearing one another in love.—Eph. 4: 1 & 2.

2. If it be possible, as much as lieth in you, live peaceably with all men.—Rom. 12: 18.

GIRLS.

1. Forbearing one another, and forgiving one another if any man have a quarrel against any: even as Christ forgave you, so also do ye.
And above all these things put on charity, which is the bond of perfectness.—Col. 3: 13 & 14.

2. Follow peace with all men, and holiness, without which no man shall see the Lord.—Heb. 12: 14.

BOYS.

1. And the servant of the Lord must not strive; but be gentle unto all men, apt to teach, patient.—II Tim. 2: 24.
4. Let us therefore follow after the things which make for peace, and things wherewith one may edify another.—Rom. 14: 19.

GIRLS.

Finally, brethren, farewell. Be perfect, be of good comfort, be of one mind, live in peace; and the God of love and peace shall be with you.—II Cor. 13: 11.
4. A word fitly spoken is like apples of gold in pictures of silver.—Prov. 25: 11.

Sing p. 92.

SUPT.—What is the next Beatitude?

TEACHER.—Blessed are they which are persecuted for righteousness' sake: for theirs is the kingdom of heaven.

SUPT.—What other words of consolation may the persecuted for Christ's sake find in the Book of Books?

BOYS.

1. Blessed are ye when men shall hate you, and when they shall separate you from their company, and shall reproach you, and cast out your name as evil, for the Son of man's sake.
Rejoice ye in that day, and leap for joy: for, behold, your reward is great in heaven: for in like manner did their fathers unto the prophets.—Luke 6: 22 & 23.
2. If we suffer, we shall also reign with him: if we deny him, he also will deny us.— II Tim. 2: 12.
3. But rejoice, inasmuch as ye are partakers of Christ's sufferings; that when his glory shall be revealed, ye may be glad also with exceeding joy. —I Pet. 4: 13.
4. But let none of you suffer as a murderer, or as a thief, or as an evil-doer, or as a busybody in other men's matters.—I Peter 4: 15.
5. For our light affliction, which is but for a moment, worketh for us a far more exceeding and eternal weight of glory.—II Cor. 4: 15.

GIRLS.

1. Remember the word that I said unto you, The servant is not greater than his lord. If they have persecuted me, they will also persecute you; if they have kept my saying, they will keep yours also. But all these things will they do unto you for my name's sake, because they know not him that sent me.—John 15: 20 & 21.
2. Who shall separate us from the love of Christ? shall tribulation, or distress, or persecution, or famine, or nakedness, or peril, or sword?
Nay, in all these things we are more than conquerors through him that loved us.—Rom. 8: 35 & 37.
3. If ye be reproached for the name of Christ, happy are ye; for the spirit of glory and of God resteth upon you: on their part he is evil spoken of, but on your part he is glorified.—I Peter 4: 14.
4. Yet if any man suffer as a Christian, let him not be ashamed; but let him glorify God on this behalf.— I Peter 4: 16.
5. Fear none of those things which thou shalt suffer: be thou faithful unto death, and I will give thee a crown of life.—Rev. 2: 10.

Sing p. 93.

ALL.—Blessed are ye, when men shall revile you, and persecute you, and say all manner of evil against you falsely, for my sake.

Rejoice, and be exceeding glad: for great is your reward in heaven.

Sing p. 94.

Index.

A little child shall lead. L. M.	20
Almost in sight. 7s & 6s.	44
Angels roll'd the stone away. (Easter.)	49
As our day. 8s & 7s.	17
As we forgive. C. M.	39
Ask and it shall be given. 7s & 6s.	72
Beautiful Angels. 10s.	47
Beautiful mansions. P. M.	65
Be not weary. 8s & 7s.	10
Be ye joyful. 8s & 7s.	9
Beyond the river. 9s & 7s.	15
Blessed is He that cometh. P. M.	3
Blessed are they that hunger. 7s & 6s.	88
Blessed are the pure in heart. L. M.	89
Blessed are the merciful. 7s & 6s.	90
Blessed are the Peacemakers. 7s & 6s	92
Blessed are they that are persecuted. L. M.	93
Blessed are the poor in spirit. 8s & 7s.	85
Blessed are they that mourn. S. M.	86
Blessed are the meek. 7s & 8s.	87
Carol, children, carol. (Easter.)	52
Cast thy burden. 7s.	30
Chants.	62
Charity. 8s & 7s	84
Christmas Bells. (Christmas.)	59
Christ is risen. (Easter.)	50
Christ is risen. (Christmas.)	57
Deliver us from evil. 7s & 6s	41
Evening brings us home. 7s & 6s	76
Faith. 7s & 6s	82
Faith keeps us thro' the day. 7s.	71
Father, take our hands. 7s.	23
Fight the good fight. 6s & 5s.	13
Folded in the Saviour's arms. L. M.	70
Forgive us our trespasses. 7s	38
For ever and ever. 11s.	43
Gather in His lambs. 8s & 7s.	14
Give. 7s & 6s.	18
Give us this day. L. M.	37
God bless our home. 7s & 6s.	46
Hallowed be Thy name. 7s & 6s.	34
Haste, ye nations. 8s & 7s.	5
He leads us on. 7s.	19
Here in love we meet. P. M (Anniversary.)	61
Here in love we meet.	66
Hope. L. M.	83
How sweet to gather. L. M.	77
I love the Sunday School. 9s & 5s.	64
In the by and by. 8s & 6s	61
In the lowly manger. (Christmas.)	54
Keep your lamps burning. 10s.	45
Late! too late. 7s.	25
Lead us not into temptation. 8s & 6s.	40
Let the Saviour in. 8s & 5s.	12
Let us fold our hands. 7s	31
Lift us up.	78
Little ones who walk in light. 8s & 7s.	80
Little pilgrims. 8s & 7s	28
List our merry carol. (Christmas.)	55
Marching to the river. 8s & 5s.	27
No Cross, no Crown. 8s & 6s.	48
O, lovely star. (Christmas.)	56
O, river of mercy. 11s.	60
On the other side. 8s & 7s.	74
Only gone before. 8s & 7s.	75
Our Father who art in Heaven. P. M.	33
Pray without ceasing. 10s.	32
Raise the banner of the Cross. P. M	8
Rest in the shadow. L. M. D.	62
Round the Christmas tree. (Christmas.)	58
Sabbath bells. 8s & 7s.	24
Scatter seed. 7s & 6s	21
Seek, and ye shall find. L. M.	81
Step by step. 7s	69
Sweet thoughts of Heaven. L. M.	16
The beautiful hereafter. 8s & 6s.	22
The gates ajar. 7s & 6s.	7
The golden city. 7s & 6s.	63
The home where Angels dwell. L. M.	4
The sparrow's fall. L. M.	29
Thine is the Kingdom. C. M.	42
Three golden words. C. M.	73
Thy Kingdom come. L. M.	35
Thy will be done. 6s & 4s.	36
Under the Cross. L. M.	67
Watch and pray. 7s & 3s.	11
We'll soon be home. 6s & 4s	26
What little hands may do. 7s.	6
When we cross the river. 6s & 5s.	79
Work in God's vineyard. 10s.	68

CHANTS.

Psalms.	94
Morning Service.	95
" "	96
" "	97
Evening Service	98
" "	99
" "	100
" "	101
Concert Exercises on the Lord's Prayer.	102
The Beatitudes, (a Concert Exercise.)	104

THE TEACHER'S FAVORITE!

—THE—

New England Conservatory

METHOD

FOR THE PIANO-FORTE,

Is being adopted by all the Conservatories and best Teachers throughout the country, and is by far SUPERIOR to all other Methods.

SURE TO MAKE GOOD PIANISTS OF ALL WHO STUDY IT THOROUGHLY!

Published in both American and Foreign Fingering.

In Three Parts. Price of each Part, $1.50, Complete, $3.75.

☞ Liberal Discount to Dealers and Teachers. ☜

C. D. Russell & Company,

126 Tremont Street, - - - - Boston.

Standard Musical Works.

Published by G. D. RUSSELL & COMPANY, - 126 Tremont Street, Boston.

PIANO-FORTE METHODS.

Carpenter's Elementary School for the Piano Forte. American Fingering.		$1.00
Carpenter's Elementary School for the Piano Forte. Foreign Fingering.		1.00
Champion Piano.	*Lazar.*	.75
New England Conservatory Method. Foreign or American fingering.		3.75
In three parts, each, Boards,		1.50

PIANO PRIMERS.

Jousse's Catechism, Burrowes' Piano Primer and Guide to Practice combined. Boards,		.35
Ditto, Cloth,		.45
Buck's Dictionary of musical terms.	*D. Buck.*	.35

ORGAN METHODS.

American Organ. Complete method for Cabinet Organ.	*Clarke.*	2.00
Home Recreations for Cabinet Organ.	*Clarke.*	1.50
Leslie's Cabinet Organ,	*Leslie.*	.75

VOCAL METHODS.

Basini's New Method,		3.00
Bonaldi's 46 Complete and Progressive Studies for vocalization. Soprano.		.75
Ditto. Contralto.		.75
Concone's 50 Lessons in Singing. Book 1. Op. 10. Book 1.		2.00
" 25 " " " " "		1.50
" Exercises in singing.		1.25
Vaccaj's Vocal Method.		1.50

CHAMPION METHODS. Without a Teacher.

Champion Piano.	*Lazar.*	.75
Champion Violin.	*Lazar.*	.60
Champion Flute.	*Lazar.*	.50
Leslie's Cabinet Organ.	*Leslie.*	.75

SACRED MUSIC BOOKS.

Carmina Alterna, A selection of Psalms for Responsive service.	*Brown.*	1.00
Chorister. For Schools, Choirs and Conservatories,	*Perkins.*	1.50
Church Roll. " " " "	*Perkins.*	1.25
Church Welcome. " " " "	*Perkins.*	1.50

Clarion. Anthems and Choruses.	*L. Marshall.*	.50
Sanctuary. Quartettes and Choruses. Cloth.	*Kreissmann.*	3.00
" " " " Boards.		2.50
Star of the East.	*A. Hull.*	.30
Sixty-seven Chants.	*Lazar.*	.30
Starry Crown of Sunday School Melodies. Boards.		.35

MASONIC.

Masonic Choir.	*J. W. Dadmun.*	.75

SCHOOL SINGING BOOKS.

Hunter's Daughter. Cantata.	*Turner.*	.15
Mettor. "	*Leslie.*	.60
Mocking Bird. For Grammar Schools.	*Perkins.*	.50
Songs of the Months. Cantata.	*Webster.*	.15
Laurel Wreath. For High Schools and Seminaries.	*Perkins.*	1.00
Seminary Album. For Female Seminaries.	*Perkins.*	1.00

GLEE BOOKS.

New Crystal Spring. Temperance.	*Whiting.*	.35
The Jewel. A Glee Book.	*Ernest Leslie.*	.75

SONG BOOKS.

Mammoth Songster.		.25

PIANO AND VIOLIN OR FLUTE.

Leslie's Duetts. Violin or Flute and Piano.	*Ernest Leslie.*	1.00
Violoncello School.	*Fries & Suck.*	3.00

COLLECTION OF PIANO MUSIC.

Beethoven's Sonatas. Two Volumes. Cloth. each,		8.00
" " " " Full Gilt. "		6.00
Fountain of Gems. Boards.	*Leslie.*	2.50
" " " Cloth.	*Leslie.*	3.00
Mendelssohn's 49 Songs without words. Cloth.		5.00
" " " " Full Gilt.		6.00
Mozart's Sonatas. Cloth.		5.00
" " Full Gilt.		6.00
Schumann's Album. 43 Piano Pieces. Cloth.		3.00
Chopin's Waltzes. Cloth.		3.50
Dexter Smith's Poems.		1.25

BASSINI'S
NEW METHOD,

A COMPLETE

COURSE OF INSTRUCTION

FOR THE

Soprano and Mezzo Soprano Voices.

This world-renowned composer and teacher of the voice has fairly outdone himself in the above Method, as this work contains all that is important in his former Methods, besides many improvements which time and experience have brought to light, making this the

Most Improved,

Most Instructive,

Most Progressive,

AND

THE BEST METHOD

For the Teacher and Pupil that has ever been published.

BY CARLO BASSINI.

Published in Large Quarto. Price $3.00.

G. D. RUSSELL & COMPANY,

126 Tremont Street, Boston.

New Book for Female Seminaries.

SEMINARY ALBUM!
For Female Voices.

This Book will be issued in a few weeks. The author has spared no pains to make it the finest work ever issued for Female Voices.

The first part is devoted to elementary instruction and vocal exercises which are arranged in a pleasing, comprehensive and progressive manner. The remainder of the work consists of a collection of Songs, Duets and Trios, all selected with great care and arranged expressly for Female Voices.

We are sure this book will find a welcome in all Seminaries throughout the country.

PRICE, $9.00 PER DOZEN.

Composed, arranged and adapted by

W. O. PERKINS.

Specimen copies, postage free on receipt of the dozen price.

NEW MUSIC BOOK
—FOR—
Female Seminaries,
High and Normal Schools
and Academies.

THE
LAUREL WREATH.

This book will be found more complete and better adapted for the use of High Schools than any work yet published; it is divided into four parts, viz:

Part 1st—Is a thorough course of elementary instruction.

Part 2d—Is a Treatise on the Cultivation of the Voice, with directions for the practice of Physical Exercises for the Development of the Respiratory and Vocal Organs, and Copious Vocal Exercises, Scales and Solfeggios for practice.

Part 3d—Contains a great variety of Select Music for Schools, Concerts and general use; mostly arranged for two, three and four Female Voices; many pieces are written for mixed voices, but are so arranged that they can be used for female voices.

Part 4—Contains Sacred Music, Anthems, Chants and Hymn Tunes.

COMPOSED AND ARRANGED BY

W. O. PERKINS.

Author of "Church Bell," "Nightingale," "Golden Robin," "Starry Crown," &c.

PRICE, - - - - - - - - $1.00

G. D. RUSSELL & COMPANY,
126 Tremont Street, Boston.

WM. A. POND & CO.,
Nos. 547 & 896 Broadway, N. Y.

www.ingramcontent.com/pod-product-compliance
Lightning Source LLC
Chambersburg PA
CBHW020141170426
43199CB00010B/832